THE ENDURING

The Antarctic Legacy of Sir Ernest Shackleton and Frank Hurley

Curated by Meredith Hooper

Syon Publishing

THE ENDURING EYE

Publisher Graeme Gourlay
Editor Paul Presley
Art Director Gordon Beckett
Based on the exhibition text, curated by Meredith Hooper

Syon Publishing, Suite 3.20, Q West,
Great West Road, Brentford, Middlesex TW8 0GP
Telephone: 020 8332 8410

Printed by Stephens & George Print Group, Merthyr Tydfil, Wales

To buy further issues to be delivered by post go to
www.syonstore.com

Contents

Foreword

Photography renders the unbelievable real. When history began to be recorded on glass plates and celluloid, humanity's most extreme endeavours gained a silent witness. Without the cameras that young Frank Hurley took south with Ernest Shackleton in 1914, the world would have struggled to believe this extraordinary story: the loss of the ship in Antarctic pack ice at a location beyond rescue, the camps on ice floes, the sled-hauling, hunger, cold and comradeship, the perilous voyages in open boats and that final, famous passage across 850 miles of ferocious sea to South Georgia and safety. Captured by Hurley on his Graflex cameras, his Paget colour equipment and his Folding Pocket Kodaks, some 259 images eventually reached the sanctuary of the Royal Geographical Society, now home to the largest private geographical collection in the world. Exactly one century after Hurley filmed the expedition's defining moment – the crushing of its ship by the earth's forces – the entire collection has now been digitised at a resolution that has never been seen before. It is as if we are witnessing one of the greatest feats of human endurance for the first time.

Nicholas Crane, FRGS
President, Royal Geographical Society (with IBG)

Introduction
The Hon Alexandra Shackleton

A hundred years ago, Ernest Shackleton and his men set forth on the Imperial Trans-Antarctic Expedition. He regarded it as the last great adventure; to cross the Antarctic from the Weddell Sea to the Ross sea via the South Pole. Two ships, *Endurance* in the Weddell Sea and *Aurora* in the Ross Sea. *Aurora* was to lay depots for the *Endurance* party.

Fortunately for posterity, the *Endurance's* photographer, the Australian Frank Hurley, was one of the greatest polar photographers ever known and it is his 'Enduring Eye' we celebrate. The Royal Geographical Society is fortunate enough to have Hurley's glass plate negatives.

Hurley was described as a 'warrior with a camera'. He was happy to climb the mast of the ship carrying the heavy brass and mahogany camera and willing to lie down in front of the moving ship. Getting the results was everything. His amazing black and white images not only provide an unrivalled record of the events of the expedition but they are astonishingly beautiful.

It is difficult to choose one's favourite image. The vision of the frost-covered ship, set against the dark, polar night is perhaps the best known. Hurley got the effect by putting 24 phosphorus flares around *Endurance* without telling his companions. She looks fairy-like in her beauty. Then there is the image of the tiny *James Caird* setting forward on her epic voyage of 800 miles across the stormiest seas in the world. Eventually, all the men of the Weddell Sea Party were rescued. Sadly, the Ross Sea Party on the other side of the Antarctic did not fare so well. Mistakes were made and three men died. We are all indebted to Hurley's 'Enduring Eye'.

Frank Worsley and Lionel Greenstreet looking down on the *Endurance* moored in South Georgia

MEMBERS OF THE IMPERIAL TRANS- ANTARCTIC EXPEDITION

Sir Ernest Shackleton, leader
Frank Wild, second-in-command
Frank Worsley, captain
Lionel Greenstreet, first officer
Hubert T. Hudson, navigator
Thomas Crean, second officer
Alfred Cheetham, third officer
Lewis Rickinson, first engineer
A.J. Kerr, second engineer
Dr. Alexander H. Mackin, surgeon
Dr. J. A McIlroy, surgeon
James M. Wordie, geologist
Leonard D. A. Hussey, meteorologist
Reginald W. James, physicist
Robert S. Clark, biologist
James Francis (Frank) Hurley, official photographer
George E. Marston, official artist
T. Orde-Lees, motor expert (later storekeeper)
Harry McNish, carpenter
Charles J. Green, cook
Walter How, able seaman
Timothy McCarthy, able seaman
William Bakewell, able seaman
Thomas McLeod, able seaman
John Vincent, able seaman
Ernest Holness, fireman
William Stephenson, fireman
Perce Blackboro, stowaway (later steward)

28 men live on board the *Endurance*. *Endurance* is their home and their transport: the means of entering – and escaping – the Antarctic ice.

1 Entering the Polar Sea

November/December 1914

During the month's wait in South Georgia, Hurley photographs and films the austere beauty of the island's mountains, glaciers and fjords.

Shackleton gets extra food, winter clothing and coal from the whaling stations in South Georgia. The unusually severe conditions rule out any possibility of crossing the continent this season.

'The space between the wardroom & the after cabin has been filled up with coal, & the only way into the wardroom is down a ladder in a hole excavated in the coal just in front of the door… All being well you should see us back in the spring of 1916,' Reginald James in a letter home, 11 November.

On the bow of the *Endurance*

'Left South Georgia on December 5th...the last link with civilization. On the third day we came into pack ice...'

Reginald W James, physicist

'The pack ice is always on the move, opening & closing...'
Reginald James, physicist

'We took from South Georgia about a ton of whale meat, food for the dogs; big chunks were hanging in the rigging out of reach but not out of sight & as the ship rolled & pitched they watched with wolfish eyes...'
Lewis Rickinson, first engineer

Endurance enters the pack ice

Frank Hurley aloft
with Shackleton on the
deck of the *Endurance*

'6 January... we were called out of bunk... at 11pm... going on deck we discovered we were in the midst of an impenetrable field of heavy pressure ice. During the day the dogs were taken for a run on the large floe... the first they have had for nearly a month'
Frank Hurley

Mast of the *Endurance* with the wake of the ship through a field of young ice

Dogs and men on the ice with *Endurance* behind

'8 January... reaching our base is far harder than anyone... expected'
Thomas Orde-Lees, motor expert

'...here we are with
the land in sight...
absolutely helpless'
Frank Hurley

Caird Coast, as seen
from the deck
of the *Endurance*

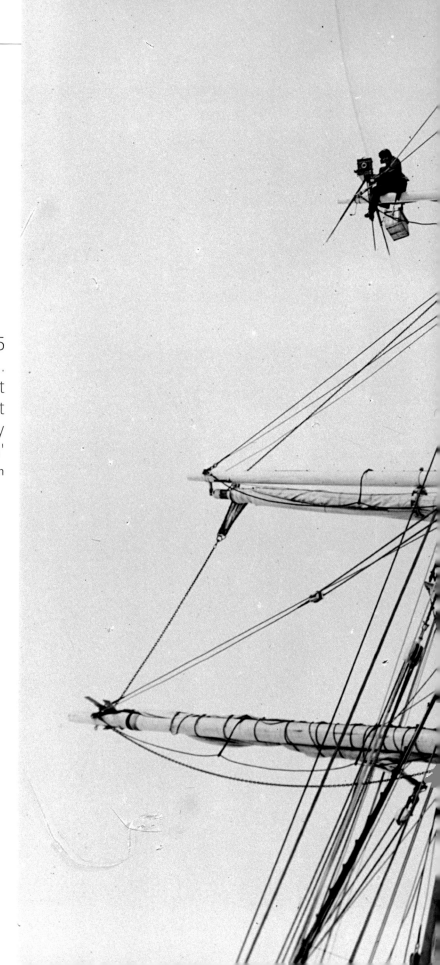

12 January, 1915
'We came across new land...
photograph was taken at
midnight – the sun is almost
as strong... as at mid-day
during the summer months'
Lewis Rickinson

24 January, 1915
'... Hurley, the irrepressible...
perched like a dicky bird
on the top sail yard arm is
taking a colour photo of ship
and ice...'

Frank Worsley, captain

Hurley filming from
the mast of the
Endurance

Endurance in full sail, in the ice

25 January, 1915
'... 3 hours unsuccessfully try to force ship... with all sails on (& engines)... Hurley goes on floe & takes a picture of ship & floe'
Frank Worsley

'... not one on board who was not bitterly disappointed'
James M Wordie, geologist

'14 February... a decisive effort...
made to free the ship...

Frank Hurley

Attempt being made to
cut the *Endurance* from
the grip of the ice

14 February, 1915

At midnight Shackleton calls a halt to a tremendous effort to cut the ship free from thick ice. The 15th, Shackleton's 41st birthday, *Endurance* – so close to where they hoped to land – is acknowledged to be trapped.

Shackleton's cabin on the *Endurance*

'a pretty despondent crowd'
James Wordie

Thomas Crean
second officer,
with puppies

'... to be on the safe side we are
now beginning to lay in a stock of
seal meat for the winter for kitchen
& the dogs'
Frank Hurley

Skinning seals
on the floe

'... all hope is not yet given up of
breaking free...'
Frank Hurley

16 February, 1915
'The Boss took... defeat very well... was in the best of spirits today and gave orders for a proper football match to take place this afternoon'

James Wordie

Football match on the ice

2 On the Drifting Sea Ice

Winter, 1915

Imprisoned in the pack ice, *Endurance* drifts. All hands are formally 'put off' ship's routine. The sailors in their quarters in the foc'sle have little to do. For Worsley, his ship becomes in effect a shore station, '… strange to hear & feel a fresh gale… & to feel absolutely no motion or even vibration in the ship. She is held rigid as a rock.'

Full polar clothing intended just for the landing party is shared out among the whole ship's company. Carpenter Harry McNish uses the timber intended for the shore hut to build cubicles in the 'tween decks for winter quarters. The dogs, transferred to specially built 'dogloos' on the ice, begin training in sledge teams. The scientists create work programmes. Hurley fits up the ship's refrigerator in the hold as a dark room. To develop his cinema films he uses a paraffin heater to keep the water from freezing.

Routine for the men is essential, as is keeping busy. 'Told off if late for meals by two mins', Worsley recounts.

For Shackleton, visible optimism is key. At the same time he exercises strict control over all movement away from the ship. McNish recounts '… no outside work only arguments about the war'.

Winter and darkness close in. '3 May… the last day on which we could have looked for the sun, but it never appeared'.

Crammed inside a wooden shell trapped in a vast ocean of ice, the 28 men are utterly alone. Out of all contact.

The scientists washing down the 'Ritz', the living quarters in the hold (left to right: James Wordie, Alfred Cheetham and Alexander Macklin)

Ice mounds and ropes
serve as guidance to the
crew on the ice in darkness
and blizzards

Frank Hurley and Leonard
Hussey engaged in a friendly
tournament

Leonard Hussey and Reginald
James taking observations

'Scientists now start to prepare
their own special work...
Imprisonment in the ice pack is
very hard on the geologist'
Frank Worsley

22 June, 1915

The day the sun begins to return – 'treated as Christmas Day… the special feast of duck and green peas, fresh – out of the tin.' Lewis Rickinson.
'After… the end of the room was converted into a stage… the footlights were of acetylene, five burners with biscuit tin lids for reflectors… everybody did something… Most of the performers were in costume.' Reginald James. Fo'c'sle members had their own celebration.

Mid-winter dinner

Life improves greatly in the Ritz after Hurley, technically resourceful, fixes up
an electric light plant. Blackboro, the steward, brings in the daily supply of water

Robert S. Clark, biologist

13 March, 1915

'Clark works dragnet... & obtains a good haul of plankton...'
Frank Worsley

Hurley and Macklin at home in the 'Billabong' — the only double cubicle on the *Endurance*, shared by Hussey and McIlroy

'The Night
Watchman's
Story' in the
wardroom (or
'Ritz') of the
Endurance

'All hands are on all day & sleep all night except for the Night Watch who looks after the dogs & ship & keeps his eyes skinned for any sign of a possible crack in the ice... from 8pm to 8am'

Frank Worsley

'The Night Watchman returns'

Checking for
specimens in an
ice hole beside the
Endurance

Frank Worsley and
Reginald James taking
stellar observations

Frank Hurley with a movie camera on the ice beneath the bow of the *Endurance*

'The charges of flash powder were
placed in three shielded receptacles
and fired electrically. The dogs were
extremely scared...'
Frank Hurley describes photographing the dogs at night

Weighing
the dogs –
once a week

Hurley feeding
the dogs
during winter

'Dogloos' – Igloo kennels built for the dogs on the ice

Harnessing the dogs to the sleds

Dog team being exercised over a pressure ridge

1 August, 1915

In winter's dark, *Endurance* drifts north. Signs of distant trouble come nearer – ice heaving up, slow masses rolling over each other. The wind howls in the rigging.

Endurance experiences her first attack. Things quieten. But pressure increases, menacing in the darkness and cold of winter.

'...the floe surrounding us started breaking up... pressure... forcing large masses of ice underneath us... all hands warned to stand by, get all the sleep they can & have their warmest clothes in readiness to 'get out and walk'... A year ago... this day and hour... we unmoored in the SW India Docks & started South'

Frank Worsley

'The long, long night'

'During night... take flashlight of ship beset by pressure. This necessitated some 20 flashes, one behind each salient pressure hummock no less than ten of the flashes being required to satisfactorily illuminate the ship herself. Half blinded... I lost my bearings... bumping shins... & stumbling into deep snow drifts... 1.30am. All hands aroused by crack starting from under mizzen chains to starboard stern. Sledges taken on board...'

Frank Hurley

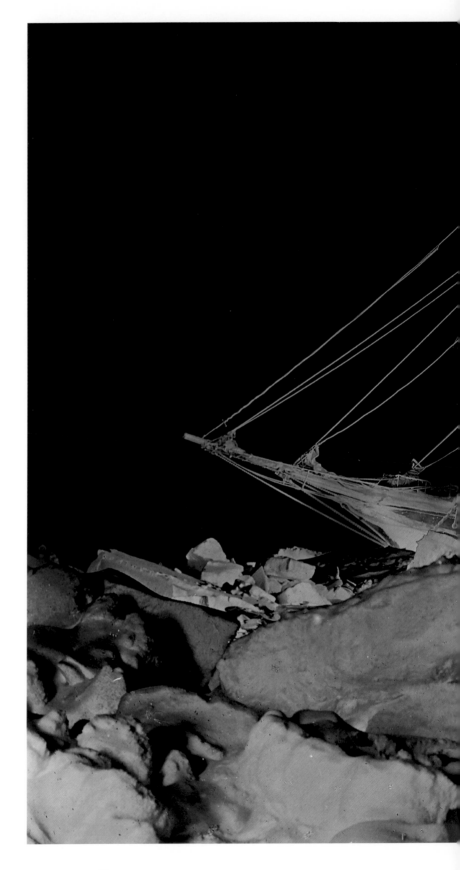

The *Endurance* beset by pack ice

3 The Returning Sun

August, 1915

The returning sun brings clear August days. Hurley ranges away from the ship with his dog sledge, capturing the clarity of light, the tones and textures of white, the chaos of ice in frozen motion. Superb evocations of the beset ship on her maiden voyage, ice-glittering; a 'Bride of the Sea' chance-placed in vast, careless spaces.

Endurance travels steadily north. In late spring or early summer perhaps she might break free of the pack. The ice might open allowing them to escape.

But always the sounds of the ice creaking, groaning, squealing, roaring: reminders of threat.

Crystal ice 'flowers' on the surface of the newly frozen ice, with *Endurance* behind

Endurance frozen in the ice

16 August, 1915
'No land in sight... a rattling good
game of hockey chased the last
lingering blue devils away... The
pack... in a state of chaos... heavy
pressure ridges in all directions'

Frank Worsley

'Dawn After Winter'. Pressure near
the ship. Blocks newly rafted up

Skiing
on the ice

A pressure ridge in formation

'The pack in a state of chaos with heavy
Frank Worsley

pressure ridges in all directions'

The *Endurance*
surrounded by
pressure ice

A crew member standing on
the ice with the *Endurance*
in the background

30 August, 1915

'Develop plates accumulated. Darkroom
work rendered extremely difficult by the
low temperatures it being –13 outside... the
darkroom situated abaft the Engine room is
raised to above freezing point by a primus
stove. A large bulk of Hypo is made into a
solution & raised to 70°. The dishes must
be warmed with the developer which is kept
reasonably constant by additions from a warm
source. Washing plates is troublesome as the
tank must be kept warm or the plates become
an enclosure in an ice block. After several
changes I place them in a rack in Sir E's cabin
– which is generally at an equable temperature.
The dry plates are all spotted & carefully
indexed. Development is a source of much
annoyance to the fingers which split and crack
around the nails in a painful manner'
Frank Hurley

The returning sun
illuminates *Endurance*
trapped in the ice

September, 1915

The members of the Endurance expedition wearing full
polar clothing and gathered under the bow of the ship

Taking the dogs out for exercise. Shackleton, Wild or Greenstreet standing, watching in descending order: Clark, Crean, Rickinson, Wordie and Marston with lead dog

Sledge party resting
on the ice

Dr Leonard Hussey and a
dog team with *Endurance*
frozen in the ice

Returning dogs to the
Endurance after exercise
on the ice

Glacier berg
and emperor
penguin

CHAPTER

4

End of the Endurance

September, 1915

Endurance is squeezed but recovers. Bursts of pressure are followed by quiet. The floe is holding *Endurance* intact, but becoming increasingly unstable.
The last day of the month the floe cracks open. Then, with no warning.

'The worst nip we have had… the decks shudder & jump… every moment it seems as tho' the floe must crush her like a nutshell' – Captain Frank Worsley.

Suddenly the pressure stops. 'At lunch we could do nothing but talk about the… chances of the ship being free… at tea we were once more… back to the chance of the ship being crushed' – James Wordie.

Early October the 'Ritz' is dismantled. Everyone moves back to their summer cabins. 'Great cleaning up Hammering, sawing – cheers, song etc' – Frank Worsley.

15 October: 'a slight bump' – and *Endurance* breaks free from the ice. She's afloat. Then the ice 'closes & holds us fast again' – James Wordie.

The floe
cracking up

17 October, 1915

Pressure starts. 'In the engine room – the weakest part of the ship – loud noises – crashes & hammerings… the iron plates on the floor buckle up & over ride…'

18 October, 1915

'At 4.45pm the floes come together… forcing her out of the ice… heeling the ship over… with a list of 30 degrees' Frank Hurley

The *Endurance* keeling over

The ship squeezed from the ice through pressure

'The deck seemed to slide away... I was carried down into a heap of dogs... about 8pm she came up right again just as rapidly as she had heeled over. 10pm All hands called to grog... the boiler filled and fire lighted... ready to steam away if any opportunity offered,' writes Reginald James.

20 October, 1915
'I'll be blowed if I want to see any more ice as long as I live!'
Reginald James

'Sea watches not appreciated by some of the staff'
Frank Worsley

'Awful calamity overtaking the ship'
Frank Hurley

23 October, 1915

Pressure begins, again focusing on the vulnerable engine room. *Endurance* springs a leak.

Fighting to the end to save their ship, they are forced, late in the evening of 27 October to abandon the irretrievably damaged *Endurance*.

Ernest Shackleton
on the deck
looking down at
the ice

'The ice drove the engine through the galley. The galley through the wardroom. A sickening sensation to feel the decks breaking up, the great beams bending & then snapping with a noise like heavy gunfire. The cabins splintered... Relentless destruction...'
Ernest Shackleton

27 October, 1915

Ejected on to the ice, a night of tension and anxiety follows. Bitterly cold, the floes cracking, forced three times to move their tents.

The first 'Dump camp' the morning after the disaster to the *Endurance*

The *Endurance* crushed by the ice packs

28 October, 1915
'Morning came in chill &
cheerless... Hurley rigged
his kinematograph getting
pictures of *Endurance* in
her death throes'
Ernest Shackleton

THE ENDURING EYE • 4

The last of the ship after being frozen-in for ten months. Hurley, Shackleton and Wild 'pay a final visit to the wreck... a pitiful sight'

91

CHAPTER

5

Ocean Camp

30 October, 1915

Stripping to bare essentials Shackleton attempts to lead his men over the pack ice to the nearest land 200 miles west. His declared aim: to get everyone safely home.

By 1 November, defeated, they scavenge what they can from the dangerous wreck and set up 'Ocean Camp' on a thick old floe.

'We are homeless & adrift
on the sea ice'
Frank Hurley

On the drifting floe at 'Ocean' Camp'. Shackleton standing by his
tent, shoulder to shoulder with his second in command Frank
Wild. Behind them, each man stands alone. Scientists and
officers are in the mid-ground, the crew at the back

November, 1915

Hurley's images showing Ocean Camp drifting slowly north, a dark
smudge in a colossal world of floating ice, evoke isolation, distance,
the smallness and vulnerability of men held in the grip of forces
over which they can have no control.

Ocean Camp – a distant view
with the wreck of the *Endurance*
just visible on the horizon

2 November, 1915
'Try & save
negatives & bared
from head to waist
probed the mushy ice.
The cases containing
the negatives in
soldered tins I located
& practically all
were intact''

Frank Hurley

9 November, 1915
'... selected the pick of
my negatives about
150 & owing to the
necessary drastic
reduction in weight
had to break & dump
about 400'

Frank Hurley

Salvaging remains of the
Endurance at Ocean Camp

The *James Caird* after strakes
were added but without mast,
on sledge

Hurley, the practical, inventive problem solver, with his portable blubber stove outside Shackleton's tent ready for whenever they 'make a move

21 November, 1915

5pm, *Endurance* finally sinks below the ice.

The King's flag flying from the look-out platform. Hurley, Wild and Shackleton standing. Hurley's remaining equipment and images stacked outside Shackleton's tent ready to move at a moment's notice

30 December, 1915

Just before Christmas Shackleton tries again to get his men west. They drag two boats leaving the third behind at Ocean Camp along with much equipment, food and clothing.

The surface is atrocious, the ice treacherous in summer's warmth. Exhausted and disappointed, they look for a solid floe to establish a new camp. In the distance the scattered remains of Ocean Camp can still be seen.

Hauling the *James Caird*

'I lay in my bag meditating the last day of the year... drifting about on an ice floe and 189 miles from nearest known land... of New Year resolutions we have none to make as there is nothing to make them for'
Frank Hurley

The temporary galley during the march west, Thomas Orde-Lees stirring, the cook Charles Green behind

26 January, 1916

'Drifting past land we could not reach. The ice too broken
to march over, yet not open enough to launch our boats'

Ernest Shackleton

'Striking camp
during the march
west' Reginald
James

Patience Camp.
Reginald James taking
observations

'... our chief need is an opening
of the ice. Our chief danger,
being carried beyond the land'
Reginald James

March 1916

Parties of men negotiate the decaying floes back to Ocean Camp, returning with food, small comforts, books and the all-important third boat. But Patience Camp tries more than their patience. The boats are packed ready to launch the moment a lead through the ice opens: yet still the ever shifting pack allows no release. The weather is wretched, dense wet fogs, snow, gales. There's nothing to do. Their floe shrinks. Seals, essential for fuel and food, are becoming scarce. The dogs are hungry. Companions, workers, but no longer of use, they are shot.

The prospect of another winter on the pack ice appals.

The sledges packed and ready

'A start made'

9–11 April, 1916

'The ice breaks up and Party take to the Boats' Frank Hurley
Approaching the open ocean the pack heaves and jostles, opens and shuts. James calculates, in this the sixth month of their journey, that they have drifted north on the floes 490, but probably closer to 1,000 miles, 'taking our windings into account…'

9 April, 1916, mid-morning, their floe splits diagonally 'right under where our tent had been… a hurried lunch, boats were got into the water and loaded… 2.30 we were in very open pack… whales blowing all around,' writes Reginald James

At last they are free. Heading for whichever land they can reach. Hurley writes 'First night on a swaying floe… cracked in halves. Rest of the dismal dark night shivering… tension & anxiety – on a par with the ship's destruction. Next night on an isolated floe… prayed to God it would remain entire… third… drifting… boats tethered together. Wet. Achingly cold… fourth… well nigh unbearable… fifth – hope all but died. Most could row no more… never do I wish to endure such a night… Dawn… a glimpse of land!'

Elephant Island, uninhabited, ice-hung.

The expedition's official artist George Marston's paintings represent the departure and first nights of the journey in three small boats, 9–11 April, 1916.

'The first night'

'The second night'

'... the pack had drifted down on top of us and we were... prisoners... in the midst of a heaving mass of close pack' Reginald James

CHAPTER

6 Elephant Island

15 April, 1916

Half-delirious, men stagger, laugh and cry. Then sleep, dead, dreamless sleep.

But their beach is insecure. Getting back in the boats they row in a blinding gale to a new camping place. Rough, bleak, inhospitable.

'Solid earth... conceive our joy'
Frank Hurley

'Atrociously cold... blizzard fury hurled gravel & ice splinters, ripping tents to shreds... not a square inch of shelter'
Ernest Shackleton

'The first land since
5 December, 1914'
Ernest Shackleton

The *Dudley Docker* reaches Cape
Valentine on Elephant Island

'A bad time... a boat journey in search of relief
necessary... no chance at all of any search being
made for us on Elephant Island'
Frank Hurley

15 April, 1916
The first hot
drink

24 April, 1916,

Easter Monday. The *James Caird* with Shackleton, Worsley and a crew of four departs. The aim – to sail 750 miles across the wildest ocean to South Georgia to get help. Frank Wild is left in command of the marooned men.

Preparing to
launch the
James Caird

The *James Caird*
enters the water

'In the event of my not surviving the boat journey... you will
do your best for the rescue of the party'
Ernest Shackleton in a signed statement before departure

Loading fresh
drinking water
to take out to
the *James Caird*.
Shackleton is in
the rear of the
Stancomb Wills

Life on Elephant Island

The two remaining boats are overturned, rested on rock walls either end and the sides closed with the canvas remains of their tents. 'Awful squalor'.

Food, watchfully shared out from expedition supplies, is boosted with whatever they catch; penguins, seals, small birds. 'We are just as hungry after meals as before', writes Hurley.

Fuel to cook meals, melt ice for drinking water and provide minimal light comes from seal blubber and penguin skins.

Boat at sea. Painting by George Marston

James Caird
and South Georgia

In their small 22 foot boat battling with winds, weather, the relentless swells, meals gulped as they crouched beneath the decking, sleep snatched lying on the hard ballast boulders, constantly wet, thirsty – uncertainty rules their every hour. Achieving South Georgia is one of the great acts of navigation, and endurance. But having rested, fed off albatross chicks, another journey must be made across the mountains and glaciers to the whaling station on the other side of the island. Leaving McNish, McCarthy and Vincent under the overturned Caird, Shackleton with Worsley and Tom Crean do it, in 36 hours.

No-one has crossed the island before.

When during the journey all seemed lost, Worsley remembered saying to himself 'What a pity. We have made this great boat journey and nobody will ever know.' But now - they can start arrangements 'for the relief of our people.'

Landing at South Georgia

15 June, 1916

The doctors Macklin and McIlroy amputate the frostbitten toes of Blackboro's left foot. Banished from the hut during the risky operation, the men shelter in a cave, passing the time cutting each other's hair.

The party marooned on Elephant Island. Hurley photographs all except Pearce Blackboro, who is confined to his sleeping bag

'Ten men perched up in the thwarts like roosters. The rest of us on the floor'

Dr Alexander Macklin

'The hut' 'the sty' 'the Snuggery'

Sketch of the hut's interior
by Reginald James

View across West Bay
from the cave beneath
Rookery Hill

'Daily hope of
the Relief ship...
What kind of ship
will come
for us?'
Alexander Macklin

Hurley with his Vest
Pocket Kodak outside the
hut. He had been able to
save only three spools of
unexposed film

Optimistic predictions that Shackleton will arrive any day to rescue them mix with uncertainty and fears. Winter comes 'hard upon us' with darkness, little to do, nowhere to go. Days of heavy snow confine all to their bags. Gales sweep down the glacier threatening the hut. 'Bored to distraction' they go through the old rounds of songs, jokes, celebrate another Midwinter's day with a concert and toasts. But proximity oppresses, repetitive habits, personal noises.

Ice covers the sea, clears, moves back in, clears again. Still – no ship.

If the *James Caird* has not survived this most risky of journeys no-one will know they are here, in this desolate place.

'A penguin can be skinned like pulling off one's vest inside out'
Thomas Orde-Lees

Gentoo penguins coming ashore, Elephant Island

'Cape Wild, Elephant
Island, where we lived for
five months' Hurley

'We are imprisoned...'
Frank Hurley

CHAPTER

7

The Rescue

August, 1916

August comes, light returning, some warmth. But food and fuel are running short. Dense pack ice fills the bays either side of the spit then briefly clears.

Watching for a relief ship alternates with speculation about what to do if no ship appears.

30 August. Lunch of boiled seal carcass is interrupted by Marston calling the magic words – 'A ship.'

'We just hurtled out of that hut… with some boots on, some off… waved… and shouted,' writes Reginald James.

Shackleton desperately anxious to get away without a moment's wait, loads men and baggage.

'Boat taking party to the
Yelcho' Reginald James

'We had to take our chance and jump... came
alongside the *Yelcho*... an ocean going tug...
clamber aboard... and started off'
Dr Alexander Macklin

3 September, 1916

Marooned men: now suddenly they are back. 'The world has altered much.' On board, they find the London newspapers. The war news appals. On Elephant Island they have been totally cut off from everything happening everywhere else in the world.'

Ernest Shackleton and
dignitaries at Punta Arenas

Party landing at Punta Arenas

The triumphant Yelcho with crew

'I have done it... not a life lost &

Ernest Shackleton to his wife Emily from Punta Arenas, 3 September, 1916

'...we have been through Hell'

EPILOGUE

Hurley's Return to South Georgia

November 1916. While in London reviewing the commercial potential for his saved film, Hurley proposed to Perris of the *Daily Chronicle*, his agent, that he would return to South Georgia to film the necessary additional 'animal life' missing from the original reels in order to increase its value for all concerned.

Hurley departed for the south once more on 15 February, 1917 – setting sail only a matter of months after his rescue with the other members of the party from Elephant Island. Arriving at South Georgia on 25 March, Hurley spent five weeks capturing additional footage and new photographs of wildlife and landscapes. Weather conditions were advanced and his work was often impeded by seasonal mists, rain and generally poor conditions, but his new photographs of South Georgia captured the dramatic beauty of its landscapes – perhaps overlooked during the *Endurance*'s first stop over at the island. In addition to his black and white images, Hurley also experimented with the Paget Process to create colour images. His diary entries from the trip recount his fascination with the tints of mosses, the intense blue translucent qualities of light playing on glacial ice and the drama of sunrise effects, providing much new visual material.

Thanks to his endeavours, Hurley's final film, released originally as *In the Grip of the Polar Pack Ice* was an instant success, making a significant contribution towards the original costs of the expedition.

Admiring an ice buttress

Whaling station
South Georgia Island

Hamberg
Glacier, Moraine
Fjord, South
Georgia Island

South Georgia –
Hamberg Glacier,
Moraine Fjord, from
the east shore
looking west

South Georgia island

Gentoo penguin on nest

South Georgia Island

Heading inland on
South Georgia Island

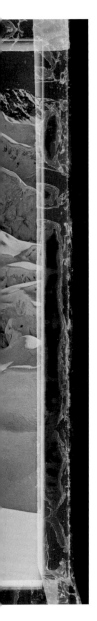

Glacier, South
Georgia Island

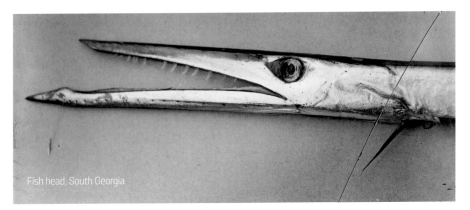

Fish head, South Georgia

Penguin rookery

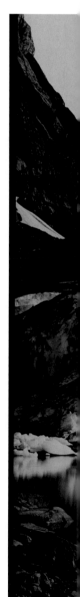

Avalanche Glacier,
South Georgia Island

Lantern Slides

The Royal Geographical Society's early contributors were originally encouraged to collect maps and books to 'advance geographical science and improve geographical knowledge'. From 1880, The *Geographical Journal* included a note asking Fellows to forward copies of photographs they had taken on their travels to the map curator of the Society. This was the beginning of the Society's unique and varied collection of photographic images, the majority of which were donated by the photographers. The Society viewed photography as an important element in all expeditions. Professor Pile, a member of the Society wrote in 1863 that 'every traveller and tourist may be his own photographer with much less trouble and difficulty than is generally supposed'. The Society created the position 'official instructor of photography' to provide technical know-how and guidance to its fellowship.

Post-expedition, many of these images were copied on to glass lantern slides to provide the returning explorers with a medium that they could project at meetings and in theatres to accompany their lectures, both to explain and illustrate their scientific reports and also for the pleasure of public audiences keen to see distant landscapes and people for the first time. Today the Society has more than 20,000 glass lantern slides held in its collections.

Frank Hurley, as the official photographer for the Imperial Trans-Antarctic Expedition was briefed to prepare duplicate sets of lantern slides for the use of many of the expedition party. One set was created for Reginald James, the physicist on the expedition, which he used in talks to illustrate his personal experience, often adding in his own slides, for example, his illustration of the blubber stove used on the ice at Ocean Camp (see page 105). In the summer of 2015, the Society was pleased to accept the gift of James' complete set of 67 lantern slides as a complement to its existing collections relating to the expedition.

Left, Elephant Island; above top, the rugged terrain on the pack ice (page 68); above, the final moments for the *Endurance*

Above, the night watch aboard *Endurance* (page 42); left the *Endurance* trapped in the Weddell Sea (page 70)

Above, pack ice appears
in the ocean

The ship stranded in a sea
of ice (page 76)

Above, the *Endurance*
crushed in the ice; right,
travelling south (page 16)

Acknowledgements

The Royal Geographical Society (with IBG) would like to thank
the following organisations and individuals

Text based on the original exhibition written and curated by Meredith Hooper, FRGS
The Enduring Eye exhibition designed by Sarner International
Epilogue and Lantern Slides, Alasdair MacLeod, FRGS, RGS–IBG

Original quotations come in almost all cases from archives held in the UK, Australia
and New Zealand and the curator and the Royal Geographical Society (with IBG) are
grateful to these organisations for the access provided.

Descriptive captions to the photographs present original RGS–IBG caption content,
some images have been deliberately cropped to enable greater detail to be shown.
Historic damage to image negatives is shown for illustrative purposes.

Landsat image mosaic of Antarctica. Image courtesy USGS, NASA, National Science Foundation, and
the British Antarctic Survey. Caption by Aries Keck.
The first high-resolution, three dimensional, true-colour map of Antarctica, released in 2007.

Supported by

The United Kingdom Antarctic Heritage Trust
Royal Commission for the Exhibition of 1851
British Antarctic Territory
Government of South Georgia & the South Sandwich Islands
Picturae
Rolex (For its support for the Society's Picture Library and contribution
towards conservation of its Collections)
Walter Scott and Partners
Heritage Lottery Fund

The Hon Alexandra Shackleton, FRGS

Associated Newspapers
British Antarctic Survey
The British Film Institute
The British Library
Buenos Aires Herald
The Daily Mirror
John Frost Newspapers/Alamy
The Royal Collection Trust
Scott Polar Research Institute
State Library, New South Wales, Australia
State Library, Victoria, Australia
Alexander Turnbull Library, Wellington, New Zealand
USGS, NASA, National Science Foundation

Miss Naomi Boneham
Ms Jan Faull
Mr John James
Mr Jonathan Marsden
Admiral Sir James Perowne KBE
Dr Carol Ann Scott
Ms Elin Simonsson
Mr Peter J Wordie
Mr Roderick Wordie, FRGS
Mrs Jane Wordie
Mr Henry Worsley, FRGS

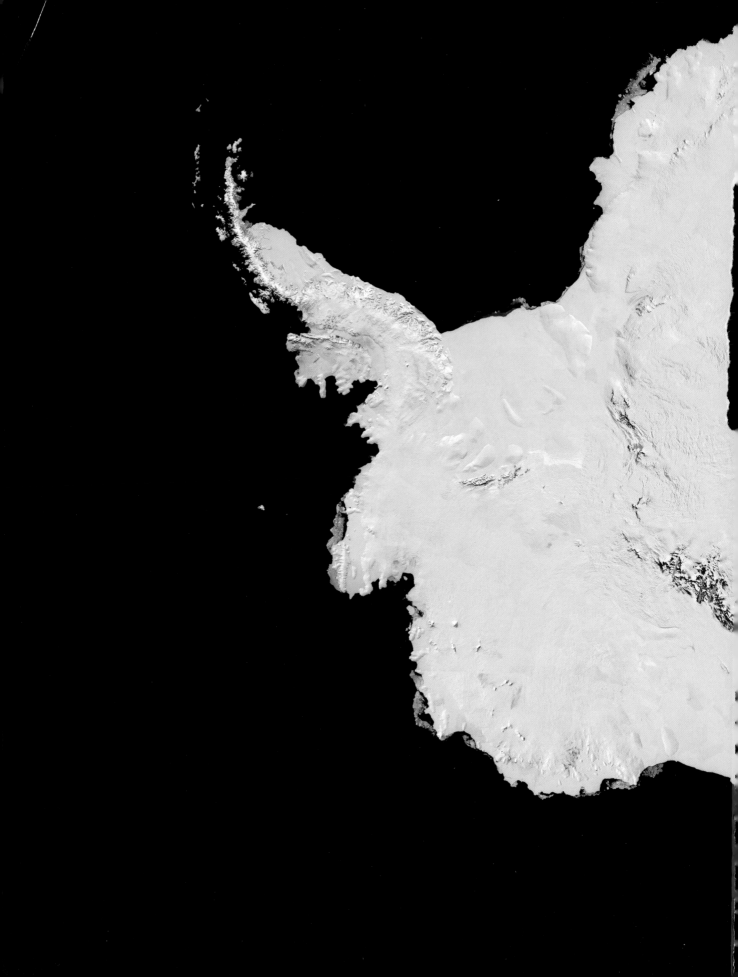